WORLD CELEBRATIONS

ROSH HASHANAH

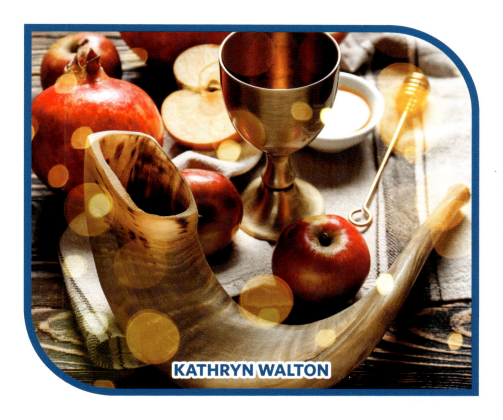

KATHRYN WALTON

Published in 2026 by The Rosen Publishing Group, Inc.
2544 Clinton Street, Buffalo, NY 14224

Copyright © 2026 by The Rosen Publishing Group, Inc.

All rights reserved. No part of this book may be reproduced in any form without permission in writing from the publisher, except by a reviewer.

First Edition

Editor: Greg Roza
Book Design: Rachel Rising

Photo Credits: Cover, pp. 1, 17 Pixel-Shot/Shutterstock.com; pp. 4, 6, 8, 10, 12, 14, 16, 18, 20 Vjom/Shutterstock.com; p. 5 simonovstas/Shutterstock.com; p. 7 Vergani Fotografia/Shutterstock.com; p. 9 Oleg Zaslavsky/Shutterstock.com; p. 11 ChameleonsEye/Shutterstock.com; pp. 13, 21 paparazzza/Shutterstock.com; p. 15 pavelr/Shutterstock.com; p. 19 rontav/Shutterstock.com.

Some of the images in this book illustrate individuals who are models. The depictions do not imply actual situations or events.

Cataloging-in-Publication Data

Names: Walton, Kathryn, 1993-.
Title: Rosh Hashanah / Kathryn Walton.
Description: Buffalo, New York : PowerKids Press, 2026. | Series: World celebrations | Includes glossary and index.
Identifiers: ISBN 9781499452211 (pbk.) | ISBN 9781499452228 (library bound) | ISBN 9781499452235 (ebook)
Subjects: LCSH: Rosh ha-Shanah–Juvenile literature.
Classification: LCC BM695.N5 W367 2026 | DDC 296.4'315–dc23

Manufactured in the United States of America

CPSIA Compliance Information: Batch #CSPK26. For Further Information contact Rosen Publishing at 1-800-237-9932.

Find us on

CONTENTS

A New Year 4
Shanah Tovah! 6
Head of the Year 8
The Shofar 10
Bread Crumbs 12
Lighting Candles 14
Special Foods 16
The Challah 18
Around the World 20
Glossary 22
For More Infomation 23
Index 24

A New Year

Rosh Hashanah is a Jewish New Year holiday. It lasts for 2 days in late September or early October. Jewish people think about the year that just passed. They think about their **relationship** with God. Many of the **customs** of Rosh Hashanah are **symbols** that have religious meanings.

Shanah Tovah!

When you think of a New Years, you might think of parties, music, and dancing. However, Rosh Hashana is a time of joyful prayer. It is a time to share joy with others close to you. People greet each other by saying "*shanah tovah,*" which means "good year."

Head of the Year

"Rosh Hashanah" is Hebrew for "Head of the Year," which means new year. It is also called the Day of **Judgement**. This means having an understanding of how God feels about you. Rosh Hashanah is also called the Day of Remembrance. This means people think about God's importance.

The Shofar

During religious services held on Rosh Hashanah, three special prayers are read. After each prayer, a religious leader blows a horn made from a ram's horn. This horn is called the shofar. It is another way for Jewish people to remember how important God is.

Bread Crumbs

Some Jewish people throw bread crumbs into a body of water on Rosh Hashanah. This practice is meant to stand for the "**casting** away of sin." It is common for people watching to shake the pockets of their clothes while this happens. This is another symbol for casting away sin.

Lighting Candles

Lighting candles for Rosh Hashanah is common. Candles are lit at the beginning of the holiday. Jewish writings say to light one candle at the start of Rosh Hashanah. Many people light two candles, and then one for every family member.

Special Foods

Meals during Rosh Hashanah have foods mentioned in Jewish religious books. People eat dates, leeks, spinach, carrots, and others foods. Before the meal, it is common to eat pieces of apple dipped in honey. This shows that people hope for a "sweet year" ahead of them.

The Challah

Challah is Jewish bread made for special holidays. On Rosh Hashanah, a round challah is made. The round shape is said to stand for the **cycle** of the year. Challah is often made with raisins so it is sweeter. People also dip challah in honey, just like apples.

Around the World

Rosh Hashanah is celebrated all over the world. The largest Rosh Hashanah celebration is held in Uman, Ukraine. In 2024, 35,000 **Orthodox** Jews gathered there! The air is filled with the sound of shofars. They gather to honor God and to celebrate this special day with each other.

GLOSSARY

cast: To throw off or away.

custom: The usual way of doing things for a person or group.

cycle: Something that repeats over and over with the same steps.

judgement: The act of judging someone, or deciding how you think about them.

orthodox: Having to do with strict religious following.

relationship: The way in which two or more people are connected.

symbol: Something that stands for something else.

FOR MORE INFORMATION

BOOKS

Last, Shari. *What Is Rosh Hashanah?* London, UK: Tell Me More Books, 2024.

Peters, Katie. *Celebrating Rosh Hashanah*. Minneapolis, MN: Learner Publications, 2025.

WEBSITES

Kid-Friendly Challah
www.pbs.org/food/recipes/challah-2
You can make this easy-to-follow recipe for challah with an adult!

Rosh Hashanah: What Is It?
www.bbc.co.uk/newsround/29363650
Learn more about Rosh Hashanah through text, photographs, and videos.

Publisher's note to educators and parents: Our editors have carefully reviewed these websites to ensure that they are suitable for students. Many websites change frequently, however, and we cannot guarantee that a site's future contents will continue to meet our high standards of quality and educational value. Be advised that students should be closely supervised whenever they access the internet.

INDEX

B
bread crumbs, 12

C
candles, 14
casting away sin, 12
challah, 18

F
family, 14
foods, 16

H
Hebrew, 8

J
joy, 6

N
new year, 4, 6, 8

S
shofar, 10, 20
shanah tovah, 6
symbol, 4, 12

U
Uman, Ukraine, 20